The
ABC's
of Living
FREE!

A 30-Day Devotional

Written by,
A. Nicole Alexander

The ABC's of Living Free
A 30-Day Devotional

Books can be ordered through booksellers or by contacting:

AleCo Enterprises LLC
1635 Old 41 Hwy NW
Suite 112-123
Kennesaw, GA 30152
(678) 822-6329
alecoplace@gmail.com

For more information, visit our Facebook page at:
www.facebook.com/alecoplace

ISBN-13: 978-0692789629
ISBN-10: 0692789626

To everyone striving to live life as an overcomer…this book is dedicated to you!

Table of Contents

Day 1
Introduction

Picture this…a man spends years of his life confined to a maximum-security prison. He adjusts his everyday idiosyncrasies to conform to what's acceptable to being behind bars and develops a certain mentality in order to survive. Many times, he will associate with a group that he feels he fits with most and those who can aid in keeping him safe and getting him the things he wants. He gets used to having to ask permission to do things that someone living in freedom may take for granted. Everything that he does is centered on thriving in the captivity that he's living in.

But then one day, he gets word that his sentence has been completed and he is being released. Immediately, he's hit with excitement at the thought of finally being free. Being able to come and go as he pleases. Being able to see loved ones he hasn't seen in years. Being able to go through life without bars being the first thing he sees in the morning and the last thing he sees at night. That excitement overwhelms him as he steps foot outside the prison walls for the first time, inhales the air of freedom and leaves his years of bondage behind.

Initially, he's able to live off of an emotional high, but as he enters a room to meet with a parole officer assigned to him, he realizes that he's not as free as he thought he would be. The officer hands him a list of things that by law he's required to do and another list twice as long of prohibitions. If that wasn't enough to burden him, he's also informed that his rights have been revoked. He can't vote in any upcoming election, he can't own certain property, he can't even go and occupy certain places. This freedom that he was so looking forward to seems to come with a higher price than he can afford to

pay. Discouragement sets in and before long, old habits from years
of captivity begin to creep in. He starts connecting with a familiar
element but the survival skills he developed in prison, don't translate
as well in a free society. He finds himself repeating the behaviors
that got him into trouble and it doesn't take long for his ways to
catch up with him and he lands himself right back behind the bars
that he thought he was forever free from. Why? Because his
mentality never changed. His body was freed, but his mind never
caught up with that freedom. He was trapped inside a mental prison
that is far more confining than any physical one. This leads him full
circle, destined to return to what he had become accustomed to.

Similar to this man, so many people struggle with things and are able
to get delivered for a season, but can't seem to stay free for a
lifetime. Matthew 12:43-45 references what happens when an evil
spirit leaves a man. The Amplified Version states:

> *"But when the unclean spirit has gone out of a man, it roams*
> *through dry [arid] places in search of rest, but it does not*
> *find any. Then it says, I will go back to my house from which*
> *I came out. And when it arrives, it finds the place*
> *unoccupied, swept, put in order, and decorated. Then it goes*
> *and brings with it seven other spirits more wicked than itself,*
> *and they go in and make their home there. And the last*
> *condition of that man becomes worse than the first…"*

When I first read these scriptures years ago, I admit I was a little
confused. I thought it was a good thing for the "house" to be swept
and clean…that meant there was nothing bad in it. Right? But it
also meant there was nothing good in it either. Not replacing the evil
with good just leaves room for the enemy to return…and not only
return, but bring reinforcements.

This is the issue that most of us face. We know how to clean the
house, but we fail to fill it afterwards, leaving us trying to fulfill
standards that we can't possibly live up to without help. We may not
deal with an evil spirit, but anything that holds us in bondage can
operate in the same manner. For some, it's an emotional prison,
others it may be mental anguish and then there are those who

struggle with a particular sin or bad habit they just can't seem to break. According to John 10:10 in the Amplified, Christ stated, "I came that they may have and enjoy life, and have it in abundance (to the full, till it overflows)." The purpose of this book is to give you the tools to refill your house so that you can attain that abundant life. A life where what laid hold of you before will never have a grip on you again. A life where you're not only free, but all your kingdom rights have been restored. Deliverance can happen in an instant, but freedom is a process. This is the beginning of your journey to living free indeed!

Throughout this devotional, you're going to be asked to take a deep look into your life and a deeper look into the life you want to have. Some things may be difficult and others may provoke emotional responses that you aren't used to having. However, if you make this commitment to yourself and to the journey before you, the things in this book will help guide and catapult you towards the life of freedom that God intended you to have. Create a prayer now and ask Him to give you the strength, wisdom and insight to do what needs to be done. Let's walk this thing out together…one day at a time.

Day 2

Acknowledge the Issue

"If we [freely] admit that we have sinned and confess our sins, He is faithful and just (true to His own nature and promises) and will forgive our sins [dismiss our lawlessness] and [continuously] cleanse us from all unrighteousness [everything not in conformity to His will in purpose, thought and action]." – 1 John 1:9 AMP

Years ago, my parents bought me a camera that I loved using to take pictures. It was the type of camera that you actually had to load the roll of film, feeding it through just right, then take it to get developed once all the pictures were taken. I would get so excited and pretty much go "snap-happy" capturing just about anything, no matter the significance. From a family member's graduation, to a butterfly that landed on a flower, even a close-up of a rock that I thought was in the shape of Texas…you name it and my camera was aimed at it.

But then one day it came time to replace the roll of film and take it to get developed. In my haste to see all the beautiful pictures I had taken, I failed to rewind the roll and opened the back of the camera, exposing the film to light. I didn't know I was doing anything I wasn't supposed to do and was devastated as the woman behind the counter at the photo print shop told me I had ruined all of my film. Every single picture, every moment that I had captured was destroyed and there was nothing anyone could do about it…all because I had exposed them to the light.

You see, your life is just like that roll of film, only it's your enemy, the devil, who is trying to develop the picture that he wants it to resemble. As long as the film is kept in the dark, he can create

5

whatever portrait he wants before you even realize it. But once you expose his film to the light, you're destroying any plan that he had in motion for your life and your future. You're cancelling his agenda.

How do you do this? We've all heard that the first step to getting help is admitting there's a problem. That's one of the most important lessons you'll learn in any twelve-step or self-help program. You can't even begin to work on an issue until you acknowledge that one exists. So many people go through life remaining in bondage because they're too afraid, too ashamed, or too proud to admit that they're not perfect and that they have a struggle. But as long as you keep the issue hidden, you're allowing that negative image to be developed and sooner or later you'll find yourself bound in a frame that's even harder to get out of.

So, what should you do? Acknowledge the issue with yourself first. Allow yourself a moment of imperfection so that you're open to receive instruction on how to make things better. Then, acknowledge the issue with God. Trust me, He already knows, but this gives Him the permission to give you the instruction on how to make things better. He's a gentleman and won't force anything on you until you're open enough to accept it. After that, find someone that you trust and acknowledge the issue with them. Whether it be a friend, a church leader, or even a counselor, someone else needs to know so that they can hold you accountable and you'll have that human help if and when you need it. Be very prayerful as to who you confide in because everyone may not be able to handle what you're dealing with. But God will place someone in your path to be there for strength, encouragement and to celebrate you on your journey to true freedom.

Your Work:

Take a moment…breathe…and acknowledge the issue(s) that you want and need to work on. Then write your own confession and declaration that you will not be bound, controlled or hindered by whatever it is anymore.

Day 3
Broken...Not Destroyed

" ...and, looking up to heaven, He gave thanks and blessed and broke the loaves and handed the pieces to the disciples, and the disciples gave them to the people." – Matthew 14:19 AMP

When I was growing up, my cousins and I would spend our summer vacations with my grandparents. We loved being there with each other, playing games, helping in my grandfather's garden, watching my grandmother can fruit and veggies, and just having a good time. For the most part, it was something I looked forward to at the end of every school year, but then there were always times when my cousins and I would get into little squabbles. The smallest things would turn into the biggest arguments but my grandmother always seemed to come up with a solution that may not have made us happy, but it was fair.

I can recall one day in particular, we were arguing over crayons. One of my cousins was using a color I wanted to use and I didn't want to wait until he was done, so I took it. We struggled back and forth trying to get the upper hand on one other over this one crayon until my grandmother walked into the room. I just knew that after I told her how long I had been waiting on that one color and how desperately I needed it in order to finish my so-called masterpiece, that she would side with me and give me the crayon. She told my cousin to place it in her hand and if I could look back, I probably had a smirk on my face because I thought I was about to get my way. But instead of taking the crayon from my cousin and giving it to me, my grandmother took it and broke it in half. I felt as if my little heart broke at the same time and I wondered why she would be so

9

cruel as to break a perfectly good crayon when she knew I was wanting to use it. But then she handed my cousin and me the pieces she had broken and told us to finish what we were doing. It was in that moment that I realized that broken crayons still color.

Too often when we are dealing with things in life, we take on the feelings of that crayon. We feel like God is breaking us in two and that there is no use for us during the process or afterwards. But just like that crayon, we are more useful to God if we allow ourselves to be broken. Unlike the negative results when people try and break us down, when God breaks us, He's doing it to get more out of us than what we realize. Just think about it…if the two fish and five loaves from the little boy's lunch in Matthew 14 had remained intact, they could never have fed a multitude of over 5000 people. Jesus had to break them in order to get more out of what was there.

So, don't fight the brokenness! Whatever you have gone through in life may have left you with some broken pieces but you are not destroyed. It's time for you to take those pieces and allow God to use them to bless others.

Your Work:

Take a look at what you think are broken pieces in your life. How can those pieces be used to benefit you and someone else? Write down your pieces and present them to God so that He can bless them and use them for His glory!

Day 4

Comfort or Progression?

"And going a little farther, He threw Himself upon the ground on His face and prayed saying, My Father, if it is possible, let this cup pass away from Me; nevertheless, not what I will [not what I desire], but as You will and desire." –
Matthew 26:39 AMP

I had a meeting on the top floor of a twenty-story building and a decision to make. Normally I would take the stairs to avoid being closed inside of an elevator, but this time it was unrealistic to think I could. So, should I deal with the temporary discomfort in order to reach my destination? Or do I skip the meeting altogether and miss a life-changing opportunity? That particular day, I chose the latter because my level of comfort was more dominant than the possibility of something greater. I allowed the fear of an elevator to keep me from what could have projected me into the future I had always wanted. But as God began to show me the intricacies of such a machine, it started to carry much more significance for me.

If asked, the vast majority of people would say they want progress in the simplest way possible. An elevator seems like the easy route to a particular place, but there are two very specific requirements for this machine to function that lead me to believe differently. The first thing you'll notice about an elevator in operation is that it cannot move until the doors are closed. In addition to the doors closing, there is always a weight capacity that cannot be exceeded. While in the natural this causes problems for people like me, who don't like confined spaces, in the spiritual it has a deeper connotation. As you progress, the capacity of past things that you'll be allowed to take with you will diminish and the door to unnecessary things in your

13

life has to be closed. The problem comes when we try to drag people and things with us because it's what we're used to and what keeps us comfortable. But in order to progress, our comfort level has to be disturbed or we'll never get off the ground.

The second feature that keeps an elevator operating properly is a pulley system. This pulley has a weight attached to it which equals the weight of the elevator when it is half full. The purpose of the weight is to make it easier for the pulley to lower and lift the elevator by providing balance. As the elevator goes up, the weight goes down and vice versa. When you think about this when dealing with the discomfort of making changes, that weight is another representation of things that have to be pulled from us in order to make progress. As we step outside of our comfort zone and into the elevator of progression that God has for us, the more weight we release, the higher we'll be able to go.

Although my initial example seemed a little extreme, how many of us miss out on opportunities to change and move forward simply because we don't want to let go of what's comfortable? You have a decision to make: comfort or progression? It doesn't have to be anything negative or wrong, but sometimes what is comfortable keeps you stuck in your current position.

Your Work:

Today you're going to release your comfort in exchange for God's progression. Write a prayer giving God permission to take you out of what you are used to and into what He has for you. He's a gentleman and won't move unless you allow Him to, so take the limits off and watch as He carries you into a freedom that you never even imagined.

Day 5

Denounce Your Past

*"Death and life are in the power of the tongue, and they who indulge in it shall eat the fruit of it [for death or life]." –
Proverbs 18:21 AMP*

Expectant parents spend days, weeks, sometimes even months trying to pick out the perfect name for their unborn child. They reference books that give the meanings of names, consult with friends and family members to get their opinions and are often found reciting the full name they've picked out just to make sure it has the right ring to it. Then the child is born and it seems that almost always, the parents will develop nicknames based on the child's personality, a shortened version of their full name or possibly some physical trait that they possess. As the baby grows and throughout childhood more and more people catch on to these nicknames to the point that the child begins to introduce themselves in that manner instead of by the name given at birth.

But then one day everything changes. Lil Johnny now wants to be called John, Maddie starts introducing herself as Madison and those ever so embarrassing nicknames that almost every person has become like nails on a chalkboard to them. They're met with some resistance when trying to retrain the people in their lives who have been used to calling them by a certain name for years. But every time a nickname is uttered, the most vigilant of individuals will be sure to correct the error. It may be a little bit of a process, but if the name is an important factor to their identity they won't mind the effort that it takes.

The same is true when dealing with the issues and struggles from your past. Many times, we accept labels from others and even place them on ourselves until we begin introducing ourselves to the world in that manner. You may not go up to someone and say "Hello, I'm a woman full of lust", but your flirtatious ways introduce you as such. No one would meet a stranger and say "Hi, my name is angry, bitter man", but it comes out the first time someone does something you don't agree with. In these instances, we reinforce the label and show the world that we have accepted it as our identity. But just as a person who no longer wants to be called by a childhood nickname, when you reach the maturity to shed those labels and get back to your true, God-given identity, you too can make that change. You too can transition from what you used to be called and what you used to call yourself, to the person that God intended you to be before you were even formed in your mother's womb. It will take some retraining of both you and other people in your life, but you can denounce your past. You may be met with some resistance from those who are used to dealing with you a certain way or in a certain manner, but you have to make this change for YOU! It's during this time of retraining that you must remember the ever-important lesson that it's not what people call you, it's what you answer to and more importantly what you call yourself. It may take some time, but if you remain consistent, eventually people will begin to address the real you that God purposed for this earth.

Your Work:

So, what name or label do you need to denounce? Create a declaration denouncing the things from your past and pronouncing the Word of God over your life. Read this declaration in front of a mirror and let it truly sink in as you journey on this road to freedom.

Day 6
Eliminate the Negative

"...let us strip off and throw aside every encumbrance (unnecessary weight) and sin which so readily (deftly and cleverly) clings to and entangles us, and let us run with patient endurance and steady and active persistence the appointed course of the race that is set before us..." – Hebrews 12:1 AMP

Have you ever watched a competitive swim meet? No matter what time of year it is or what the weather's like outside, these swimmers will take their marks for the various races wearing next to nothing. They shed their street clothes and athletic jumpsuits because they know the excess attire will weigh them down in the water. The suits that they wear are specifically designed for the water and if you speak with some of the more serious aquatic athletes, they'll tell you that they even go as far as shaving all the hair off their bodies in an effort to create a smoother surface. Anything to give them a competitive edge, they are willing to try.

Now it seems like common sense that one wouldn't jump into a pool fully dressed, but so often we try to swim our way through life while carrying a load we were never meant to carry in that context. Some Christians believe that as long as they aren't breaking any of the Ten Commandments that they're not doing anything wrong. But there are some things and even some people that weigh us down that may not have anything to do with the practice of sin. It could be something that caused deep hurt decades ago that's preventing you from moving forward. Or maybe it's an "I'm sorry" that you never got to say to a loved one before they passed away, that's haunting your mind and thoughts. It could be anger, unforgiveness, or even self-hatred. All these things take root in our spirits and will eventually become the boulder that sinks us to the bottom of the sea of life. But it's completely up to you whether you want to sink or swim. Whatever it is that's holding you back and weighing you down, it's time to shed the excess baggage so that you can live free!

Your Work:

For this exercise, I want you to do something a bit different and go on a little field trip. Go to a local store where you can purchase a cheap helium balloon and a marker. Once you have the essential supplies, find a park or somewhere quiet with an open view of the sky. Get to a secluded spot and spend some time searching yourself, talking to God and listening for His input on the negative things you need to eliminate from your life. As you are led, write each of those things on the balloon, using as much space as you need. Don't rush through it, but take this reflective moment to really get everything out.

When you finish writing, take one last look at your balloon and every word that you wrote on it. Take a deep breath and as you exhale, release the balloon and everything that's been weighing you down and preventing you from living the life that you want to live...the abundant life that God intended you to live. As the balloon floats away, determine within yourself that you will never be bound again, your progress will never be hindered and freedom is yours!

Day 7

Face the Mirror

"Therefore, since we are justified (acquitted, declared righteous, and given a right standing with God) through faith, let us [grasp the fact that we] have [the peace of reconciliation to hold to enjoy] peace with God through our Lord Jesus Christ (the Messiah, the Anointed One). – Romans 5:1 AMP

I've always heard it said that unforgiveness is like ingesting a poison and expecting it to hurt someone else. But what happens when the person that you can't seem to forgive is the one whose image is staring back at you when you look in the mirror? What is a mirror anyway? Taking a deeper look into what it actually does gives a fresh perspective on forgiving yourself, no matter what wrong you've done.

To understand a mirror, we must first understand the concept of the conservation of energy. This concept mandates that energy cannot be created or thrown away, but at best, can only be converted into something else. Your body is constantly emitting light, which is energy traveling at a high speed. Any time light hits an object, one of three things will happen: the light will pass through if the object is transparent, it will be absorbed if the object is dark colored, or it will be reflected if the object is shiny enough. Whatever happens, the energy that you started with will always equal the energy that you end with.

So, what does that mean in the realm of unforgiveness? Everything you carry is the energy you emit. Whatever happened in the past is a part of that energy and cannot be recreated or destroyed, only changed into something else. As you go through life, you have three choices. You can pretend things didn't happen and it's like standing in front of a transparent object. Although you may not recognize the impact you're having, everything you emit is being transferred onto other things and other people. They're receiving all that energy, all that pain and no one is the better for it. The second choice you have is to become absorbed by your pain. In doing this, what's in front of you is dark, you can't see the light of day and you allow things from your past to consume you. Everything you do becomes about everything that was done. Your image disappears in the opaqueness of your view and the light you once had is no longer visible. But the third choice is to face the mirror. The only control that you have over the energy that's already present is to reflect it. You control what the mirror sees, therefore you control what it reflects. In facing the things that have happened, accepting that they took place, but refusing to let them control your life, you are reclaiming the power that God gave you and will be able to move forward in the dominion he predestined you to have.

Your Work:

Today it's time to rest in the peace of God and His justification by forgiving the person in the mirror. Get a pen and piece of paper and write a letter to yourself. In this letter, release everything that you need to release and make the decision to forgive everything in the past that has been holding you back. Remember, forgiveness doesn't mean it never happened, it simply means you will no longer allow the past to affect your present or your future. You have to let yourself off the hook if you truly want to live in freedom. Jesus thought you were worth forgiveness and its time that you think the same.

Day 8

Get to the Root

"Have the roots [of your being] firmly and deeply planted [in Him, fixed and founded in Him], being continually built up in Him, becoming increasingly more confirmed and established in the faith, just as you were taught, and abounding and overflowing in it with thanksgiving." – Colossians 2:7 – AMP

Knowing the what is a good thing…but knowing the why is a revelation that opens up an entirely different world of understanding.

A man planted an orchard of apple and orange trees and every year his fruit was among the top selling items at the local farmers' market. He took pride in providing the town's people with the most delicious produce, but one year something was different and numerous customers became ill. Since the customers had purchased both apples and oranges, no one could pinpoint exactly which fruit had made them sick. The man began to separate his harvest in an effort to isolate the issue and those who only bought oranges seemed to be fine while those who only bought apples continued getting sick. At first he thought something may have gone wrong with the formula he used to clean the apples before taking them to the market, so he made a few adjustments but the same thing happened with the new batch. So, he decided to take a closer look at how he treated the soil. He tried changing the fertilizer and how often he watered the orchard, but after months of waiting for the apples to ripen, he still produced a harvest of bad fruit. Out of frustration over the loss of income and still not knowing why his apples were making people sick, the man decided to dig up his apple trees and just start over with new seeds. It was during his process of digging that he noticed

29

the roots of all the trees had begun to decay as a result of root disease and from there he was able to treat the real issue and save his future harvests.

The man with the orchard knew what was happening, but it wasn't until he discovered why it was happening that he was able to change the outcome. The same thing is true when you're trying to remain free from something that has held you in bondage for any amount of time. You can change your outward behavior and even develop coping skills to help you react in a different way. But until you get to the root of why you react in a certain manner or why a particular thing affects you the way it does, you will never truly be free.

Your Work:

For this exercise, things will be a little bit different. You may be able to identify the root cause of negative behavior without prolonged thought, but for some it may require a more in-depth process. So, first, take some time to write down the things that you know are holding you back from the future you want. After you've written those things down, list your earliest memory associated with them and the feelings you had during those experiences. Some may be more difficult than others, but dig deep and really examine your thoughts, your emotions and your environment. Lastly, write a prayer asking God to reveal the connection between the things that hold you hostage and the feelings that go along with them. Ask Him to uncover what lies beneath the issues and how to address them accordingly. Pay attention and as God shows you what you need to see, come back to your list, cross out each item, and use it as another step towards your freedom.

$\mathcal{D}ay$ 9
Healing for Your Soul

"Come to Me, all you who labor and are heavy-laden and overburdened, and I will cause you to rest. [I will ease and relieve and refresh your souls.] Take My yoke upon you and learn of Me, for I am gentle (meek) and humble (lowly) in heart, and you will find rest (relief and ease and refreshment and recreation and blessed quiet) for your souls." – Matthew 11:28 AMP

We've all heard the adage that time heals all wounds. So, imagine two individuals walk into a medical facility, one with a scratch and the other with a bullet wound. The doctor comes in to see them, examines their injuries and sends them both home with a prescription to wait and let time heal their respective ailments. A few days go by and the person with the scratch looks down and barely notices that any blemish had ever been on their skin. That person goes on without a second thought or any trace that their injury occurred, but the person with the bullet wound isn't so lucky. During their time of waiting, the pain becomes unbearable. They experience internal bleeding, infection sets in and when they finally return to the hospital days later, they are at the point of death. It is then that extraordinary measures have to be taken in order to save this person's life and what should've been handled differently from the beginning is now becoming a life-altering ordeal that could've been prevented.

This seems like an extreme example but it happens to be very relevant. Pain in the physical body is an indicator that there's something wrong that needs to be addressed. Whether it's a simple issue or something that calls for more intensive medical treatment, neither instance should be ignored. The same is true with our emotions. When we experience pain, it's our mind and emotions' way of telling us that something is wrong and needs our attention. If we leave it unattended it will eventually lead to an infection that will jeopardize our well-being, our relationships and even our future. Many people think that admitting emotional pain is a sign of weakness, so they just bury it in hopes that it'll eventually go away. But just like someone who experiences organ failure due to a traumatic injury, it almost always shows up in another area of your life.

Your Work:

In order to be free in the truest sense of the word, you have to deal with the hurt that things from the past have caused. So, now's the time that we visit the emotional urgent care. The first thing you need to do is identify the symptoms that you're experiencing as a result of an event or events that took place in your life. The last chapter may help you pinpoint some things, but keep in mind, emotional pain can manifest in different ways. As you list these symptoms, create a declaration for each one, declaring that you will no longer allow that thing to infect your life. In each statement, apply the healing power of the word of God to the issue and most importantly, allow yourself the time for that healing to take place. Like any physical wound, you wouldn't expose it to an environment that may cause more damage, so the same needs to be true of your heart and emotions. Give yourself permission to take the time you need for God to make you whole and the healthier you become mentally and emotionally, the more freedom you'll be able to experience.

Day 10
Reading and Reflection

Read Psalm 91 in its entirety. Afterwards, use this page as a journal
entry to record your thoughts about this chapter and what it means to
you.

Day 11
Into the Flow

"And I am convinced and sure of this very thing, that He Who began a good work in you will continue until the day of Jesus Christ [right up to the time of His return], developing [that good work] and perfecting and bringing it to full completion in you." – Philippians 1:6 AMP

I'm driving down a side road preparing to merge onto the interstate. There's no certain time I have to be anywhere, so I didn't get frustrated when, all of a sudden, traffic came to a standstill. I was relaxed for the first couple minutes, just jamming to the music I had blaring and enjoying the beautiful day. But after another minute or two went by and traffic had only moved a few feet, I began to get concerned. I hadn't heard of any construction planned for this part of the highway, so I assumed someone must've been involved in an accident. I started praying that no one was seriously injured and as I was praying, traffic moved another few feet. I could actually see the cars on the highway now and they were at a bumper to bumper halt as well. Whatever was going on had to be pretty serious because this 70mph road had been reduced to vehicles traveling at about a tenth of that speed. We continued this crawl for what seemed like forever, until I could finally see what the issue was. It wasn't construction or some massive accident that had traffic backed up. No! On this beautiful Saturday afternoon, I had the great misfortune of being stuck behind a line of cars whose drivers didn't know how to properly merge into the flow of traffic.

Going back to my days of driver's training, I can recall my instructor explaining the purpose of an interstate onramp. The reason the ramp is so long is to give the driver trying to merge onto the expressway time to match their speed with the flow of traffic. The problem arises when someone gets to the end of the onramp and stops. They know where they want to go, they know they have to move forward, but because of fear, anxiety or sometimes lack of training, they come to a halt. Not only does this put them in a dangerous situation, but it also blocks the progress of the people coming behind them and puts them at the mercy of someone already on the highway to slow down enough to let them in, causing that traffic to become congested as well.

So, what does this have to do with the journey you're on now? Many of us get discouraged, distressed and even depressed when we want to do something different, simply because we don't know how to get into the flow and invest in the future we want to have. We know where we want to go, we know we have to keep moving forward, but because of fear, anxiety or lack of training, we stop dead in our tracks. Then, just like on a highway, we block those coming behind us and sit and wait for someone else to make a way for us. But you already have everything within you to take the first step.

Your Work:

If you want a life of freedom, it's time for you to invest in it. It's not enough just to say you want more if you never go after it. So today, whatever your issue has been, take a peek into a future without that issue and device a plan of what it's going to take to get there. Once you have that plan in place, choose one thing that you can do in the next month to begin the process. Yes, you may be fearful. No, you may not have all the resources you think you need. But, God has given you a power within, that if you tap into Him, He will direct you into the flow. No more waiting! The time is now!

Day 12

Jonah Must Go

"Do not be so deceived and misled! Evil companionships (communion, associations) corrupt and deprave good manners and morals and character." – 1 Corinthians 13:33 AMP

A lot of times we wonder why storms are raging in our lives and we can't seem to stay free, especially when we're doing everything we know to do in the will of God. In situations like these, it's helpful to take another look at the story of Jonah from a different perspective.

In Jonah's disobedience and running from God, he boarded a ship with people who were simply trying to help him get from one place to another. Little did they know that by helping Jonah, they were putting themselves in a direct path of a storm sent by God to get Jonah's attention. As the story goes, there was a terrible tempest that began to tear through the ship and the mariners tried everything in their power to make it to dry land. They began crying out to their gods and even throwing vital supplies overboard, but to no avail. They finally woke the sleeping Jonah and asked him to call on his god as well. When Jonah became aware of what was going on, he knew that the only way to save the ship was for the mariners to throw him overboard. They couldn't believe what they were being told and refused to throw Jonah off the ship because they didn't want his blood on their hands. After the storm grew worse, they determined that they had to do as Jonah had suggested and throw him overboard. As soon as Jonah hit the water, the storm ceased, the winds calmed and the ship was able to function normally.

43

So, let's pull out a couple of points from this story. First off, people that are running from God or being disobedient to what God told them to do KNOW IT, but they don't mind involving other people to try and escape what they're supposed to be doing. These types of people are detrimental to those who are trying to maintain a life of freedom.

Secondly, when the storm came, the mariners were putting themselves in danger by getting rid of their supplies (food, water, tools) in an effort to right the ship. But where was Jonah? ASLEEP! When we try to help people who God didn't intend for us to help, we put ourselves in hardship while they get all the comfort.

Lastly, after Jonah was thrown off the ship, in God's love for him, He has already prepared a large fish to come along and swallow him so that he wouldn't drown. A lot of times we feel like if we're not there to step in and help someone that they'll end up being destroyed. But God, in His infinite wisdom and love, had made provision to save Jonah and get him into a position to hear from Him.

So, on your journey to living free indeed, take time to check your ship (friendSHIP, relationSHIP, companionSHIP) and see who's on board. If there's a storm raging in your life and it doesn't seem to be letting up after your prayers, it may be because there's a Jonah on your ship that you need to toss overboard.

Your Work:

I won't ask you to make a list of people with whom you need to disassociate, but instead write out some things that you need on your ship to maintain a healthy course. As you continue in freedom, examine that list and make sure those riding with you are not being a hindrance, but rather a force that pushes you in the right direction.

Day 13
Know Your Role

"So we, numerous as we are, are one body in Christ (the Messiah) and individually we are parts one of another [mutually dependent on one another. Having gifts (faculties, talents, qualities) that differ according to the grace given us, let us use them…" – Romans 12:5-6a AMP

There are several different positions on a basketball team in which players excel based on their ability and body type. The point guard is usually the shortest and fastest on the court and is responsible for calling the plays and distributing the ball. The shooting guard is a little taller and is the most accurate outside shooter. The wing guard/small forward is a decent shooter and has a physique that allows them to play in a guard position as well as in the paint when necessary. Your power forward is tall and has a stocky build that makes them a force to be reckoned with down low. Then you have the center, who's usually the tallest on the court and the dominating presence in the post. All these players make up a complete team and the success of that team depends on how each player manages their role.

Any good youth coach would teach every player all of the different positions so they have the knowledge starting out. But as the players continue to grow into the bodies they were genetically designed to have, the coach then begins to develop the specific skills they'll need for the position that suits them. When I played basketball in middle school, I wanted to play a post position because it looked more fun and physically challenging than just passing the ball around as a guard. So, one day I asked the coach if I could spend my practice time with the "bigs" to show that I could play the position. With my five-foot frame, I went after the biggest girl on our team and repeatedly got my shot blocked, got backed down in the post, and even run over a couple of times. I found myself getting upset, doubting my ability, and even jealous of the other girl because I had the perception that she was better than me. But it was all because I was out of position. I wasn't built to be a post player, so there's no way I would succeed in such a role. I had to find the position I was built to play, develop those skills, and contribute to my team in that manner.

You may ask what this has to do with a life a freedom, but too often we fall into bondage because we're trying to fit where God never intended. We constantly compare ourselves to others and feel inadequate based on man's measuring stick. It becomes easy for us to get upset, jealous and even resentful towards someone who's succeeding in their position, when we're not operating in the one for which God perfectly designed us. Those feelings can become internalized, leading us to question our purpose, our effectiveness and the impact that we make. But when we learn to accept the position that God has for us, we can develop the abilities and skills that coincide and truly become an asset in the world we live and in our own minds.

Your Work:

For this chapter, I want you to think about you. Think about all the things that make you you and the good qualities that God invested in you. Make a list of those qualities and write a prayer to God that He will show you how to use them like only you can. There is only one you on this earth and there is a purpose for God putting you here. Let this exercise point you in the direction of that purpose and be the best you that you can be.

Day 14
Leave Your Tag On

"I will praise You, for I am fearfully and wonderfully made; Marvelous are Your works, and that my soul knows very well." – Psalms 139:14 NKJV

I can remember the first time I read it and got a little nervous, "Under penalty of law, this tag not to be removed". I didn't understand what the big deal was. Why would the police care about people removing a mattress tag? I went on for years accepting the fact that it was a law but never knew why until recently when I actually looked into the reasoning behind it.

You see, the tag on a mattress or pillow serves as the manufacturer's certificate of authenticity of its materials. This tag gives consumers a better understanding of the product based on the materials that it's made of and allows them to truly appreciate its quality. The law was put into action due to unethical merchants altering the tags so that they could put their own price on the product. They would deceive consumers and trick them into devaluing certain items or placing more value on items with lesser quality. To prevent this from occurring any longer, the law was established that only the consumer, after paying the price for the mattress, could legally remove the tag.

What happens quite often to many people is they lose a sense of their true value because they lose touch with the quality that their manufacturer put in them. Due to something that someone else has said or done, a character flaw, physical imperfection or even a shortcoming or sin that's been committed, they allow their creator's tag to be removed and the love that they should have for His product

51

is diminished. But the great thing that I've learned is, just because the tag isn't there, doesn't change the manufacturer's view of what He made. We beat ourselves up based on the things that we've done, but God continues to love us based on what He knows He placed in us. We were made in His image and there's nothing that could ever separate us from His love. The important thing to remember is, God knew before the foundation of the world that you would do what you've done, say what you've said and make the mistakes that you've made, and He still loved you enough to send His Son to pay the price for you because of the quality within you. So, in order for you to get a full grasp of what you're worth, you can't let anyone or anything remove your tag. It's not for the manufacturer to see, because He will always know His work, but it serves as a reminder to you of what you're made of so that you can know the value and fall in love with the product.

Your Work:

In the last reading, we focused on knowing and appreciating your gifts, talents and the role that you play in life and the kingdom of God. Now it's time for you to understand the quality that you're made of and fall in love with one of God's greatest creations, YOU. This isn't in a self-centered way or a manner that plants the thought that you're superior to anyone else. However, in order to walk in freedom and fulfill your purpose, you have to love yourself. Take a few moments and create a declaration expressing the materials that you're made of. In this declaration, reaffirm God's love for you and make a vow that you will love yourself no matter how outside sources may attempt to deceive you by removing your tag. Silence any voice that isn't from God and move forward in peace, joy and love!

Day 15
Mind-Field Tactics

"For I do not understand my own actions [I am baffled, bewildered]. I do not practice or accomplish what I wish, but I do the very thing that I loathe [which my moral instinct condemns." – Romans 7:15 AMP

For decades in many countries, landmines were used as one of the deadliest weapons of warfare. Armed forces would strategically place these devices, creating minefields that would prevent their enemies from passing through particular areas. The more commonly used, anti-personnel landmines, were placed just underneath the ground's surface and concealed with grass, foliage and even snow. As foot troops would attempt to cross a terrain, they would unknowingly step on the device, triggering the explosive mechanism that had the ability to maim and cause death in as far as a two-hundred-yard radius in some cases.

While this was an effective tactic during periods of war, the problem arose when wartimes ended and the landmines were forgotten. Thereafter, countless, innocent civilians would be injured and killed because they would enter these minefields without knowing the triggers were present or where they were located. Due to the loss of so many lives, governments banned the use of landmines and mandated the demining of fields as much as possible. In order to complete this task, technicians would go through the fields, one small section at a time, and use metal detectors to pinpoint where the devices were so they could be detonated safely and the field could be declared clear.

This applies in various ways when dealing with issues in the emotions and mental struggles. How many times have you flown off the handle at someone and didn't see it coming? Have you ever had a breakdown over something simple and had no idea why? Or maybe you've caught yourself doing something that you said you'd never do again and didn't understand the motive? There are so many people being blindsided by metaphoric explosions simply because they don't know what their triggers are. For some, it may be something external like the gravitational force of a full moon or the change in seasons, while others may have an internal catalyst like the reminder of a past event or a certain insecurity that sets things in motion for a major blowup. Whatever the case, it's the enemy's job to conceal these triggers to the point that we're not paying attention as we walk through everyday life. We don't recognize that we've stepped into a detrimental situation until it's too late and we're already overwhelmed or lose a part of ourselves as the result. It is therefore up to us to identify what has the potential to cause a mental or emotional explosion so that we can diffuse it before it detonates and causes damage to our well-being or any innocent bystanders.

Your Work:

Make the decision today to begin demining your mind-field. It all starts in the mind and you have the power to eliminate what was put in place to destroy you. Focus in on your thoughts, your emotions and your behavior. For everything that causes an uproar in your life or sets you in a direction that you don't want to travel, examine the inner surroundings and find the trigger. Write these triggers down and pay very close attention during the times that they occur. Only then will it be easier for you to change those thoughts, emotions and troublesome behavior and ensure that the path to your life of freedom is clear.

Day 16

New Normal

"Jesus said to him, Get up! Pick up your bed (sleeping pad) and walk! Instantly the man became well and recovered his strength and picked up his bed and walked..." – John 5:8-9 AMP

In the fifth chapter of John, we learn about the pool of Bethesda. This pool wasn't one in which people just enjoyed a leisurely swim, but there was something very special about it. At certain times of the year, an angel would come and stir up the waters of this pool and whomever stepped in first, would be healed of anything that was ailing them. As you can imagine, the pool was surrounded by people with all kinds of illnesses...some were blind, some crippled and some even paralyzed. One day Jesus encountered a certain main who was described as an invalid who had been dealing with his infirmity for thirty-eight years. When asked if he wanted to be healed, he responded that he had no one to put him in the water and that someone would always step in before him when he tried. Jesus goes on to heal him, but I couldn't help but raise an eyebrow to this story when I read it and this particular man's response.

When I think about this man's condition, the first question that comes to my mind is: How many times in thirty-eight years did he actually try and get in the pool? I can understand the first few times that the angel troubled the waters, maybe the man didn't quite know what to expect. People were probably pushing each other over with no regard like a Black Friday sale at a major department store. But after seeing the fiasco and dealing with his infirmity for, let's say five years, it seems that he would've developed a strategy for getting in the water. So, my next question is: How long did it take for him to stop trying? By the way he responded to Jesus' question, it appears to me that at some point this man accepted the issue as his normal and became content with watching others get their healing and breakthrough. He didn't even tell Jesus that he wanted to be healed, but rather gave an excuse as to why he remained in his current condition. He was fortunate that Jesus chose to heal him anyway and he was able to leave with a testimony and a new lease on life.

But how many of us are like this man and get to a point where we just accept certain issues as our normal? We deal with things for so long that they become a part of us and we forget how to function without them. We become comfortable with what we know and the thought of doing something different can even spark anxiety and fear of the unknown. It's like a child playing on monkey bars who isn't going anywhere. Many of us would rather stay stuck, holding onto that one bar, instead of reaching out for something else and moving forward. That fear of falling leaves us in a paralyzed state…sitting by a pool that could bring about the needed change in our lives.

It's time to develop a new normal. It's your turn to pick up your bed and move forward. No longer will you hold onto an issue just because it's familiar, but it's time to challenge yourself to establish a new way of living.

Your Work:

Take a moment to think about how you *used* to handle and react to certain things. Once you've gotten some examples in mind, write a series of "I will" statements that can help you do something different when the situation arises again. Meditate on your words and use these statements to fuel your journey to freedom.

Day 17
Open Your Mouth

"So be subject to God. Resist the devil [stand firm against him], and he will flee from you." – James 4:7 AMP

A man visited a tropical island and wanted to see some of the sights known only to the natives, so he hired a tour guide to show him around. They spent the day going all over the city and visiting smaller towns with historical significance. The tourist was in awe of the beauty around the island and filled the conversation with questions in order to gain more knowledge and understanding.

Towards the end of the tour, they visited a town that wasn't quite as beautiful as the other sights they had seen that day. The buildings were in ruins, there were abandoned cars scattered throughout the streets and the whole place seemed to be void of all human life. When the tourist asked his guide what had happened, the guide explained that the island was prone to devastating storms and this town had fallen victim to a massively fatal hurricane some decades earlier. Numerous questions followed and the tourist wanted to know what if anything had been done since this tragic storm to prevent something similar from happening again.

The guide proceeded to tell the gentleman about the storm siren that had been installed on the island since that deadly hurricane. In the event of an approaching storm, an alarm would sound that could be heard from anywhere on the island. This alarm signaled to the inhabitants that danger was approaching and that they should take precautionary measures immediately. The only problem with the siren was that it was so loud it was known to burst eardrums and cause severe auditory damage. To prevent this from happening, when the people heard the alarm, they had to open their mouths to balance out the pressure of the tubes in the inner ear and keep their eardrums from rupturing.

So how in the world can this principle be applied to the journey you're on? Well the enemy is very cunning and loves to fill your ears with negativity and deception. Read the passage in Matthew 4:1-11 about when Jesus was tempted by Satan in the wilderness. What did Jesus do? Did He sit and just listen to the things the devil was telling Him? NO! He opened His mouth and spoke the word of God, against which the enemy has no defense.

Too many people sit idle when the devil begins to speak things to their minds. With their mouths closed, their inner ear is filled with nonsense which eventually deafens them to the voice of God. But that damage can all be prevented in your life simply by opening your mouth and speaking the word of God!

Your Work:

Sit for a moment and think of some things the enemy has said to you lately. The Bible tells us that he is the father of lies, so we know anything he says is at best a partial truth, which is still a whole lie. Write those things down, then write and focus on the opposite, which is God's truth for your life. The next time any of those negative things try to creep into your mind, look back on this chapter and open your mouth. Declare God's word over your life, resist what the enemy is trying to tell you and he will have no other choice but to flee from you. There's no room for a devil on your journey to living free.

Day 18
Push Through

"I have strength for all things in Christ Who empowers me [I am ready for anything and equal to anything through Him Who infuses inner strength into me; I am self-sufficient in Christ's sufficiency]." – Philippians 4:13 AMP

The science class watched eagerly as the first chick began to hatch. They had adopted the clutch after the mother abandoned the nest and couldn't believe they were actually going to witness a baby bird being born. The chick seemed to be struggling to make its way out of the shell, so one of the students reached out to give it a helping hand. Immediately the teacher intervened and made sure no one touched the eggs and it led to a lesson on the importance of letting the chicks hatch on their own.

Usually an hour before the internal clock of an unborn bird triggers them to begin the hatching process, they develop what's known as an egg tooth. This egg tooth forms around their beak and is hard and sharp enough to create a crack in the protective shell in which they've been growing. This added feature, along with a strong pipping muscle in the neck, gives the chick the strength needed to hatch, although the process is gradual and can take hours. During these hours, the circulatory and respiratory systems of the bird are adjusting to the environment outside the egg and completing their developmental process which is vital for life. If the chick is helped out of the egg, its muscles won't form properly, its beak may be calcified, the sudden change in environment is too much for the circulatory and respiratory systems to support, and if the vessels attached to the shell membrane are severed prematurely, the hatchling can bleed out and die. So, while it may be tempting to offer aid, if the chick is going to live, it cannot depend on the help of others.

Moral of the story? Many people remain in bondage because they're waiting on someone else to come along and lend a helping hand. They stay stuck because they're hoping for some trigger or significant event to take place before they take the first step towards the future they want. But God is waiting on YOU! He's waiting on YOU to make the decision. He's waiting on YOU to take that first step. God wants to see just how much YOU want to live. He's already given you all the tools and strength that you need, so how badly do YOU want to be out of that shell?

He's not being cold and heartless and leaving you alone in your situation…He's not capable of doing that. But He will not force His will on anyone…you have to make the first move. Then just like the hatchling that needs care and nurturing once out of the shell, God will send the help that you need once you make the decision to be free.

Your Work:

In this moment, purpose in your heart that you will no longer wait on someone or something else to determine when your breakthrough occurs. Take the bull by the horns and stand on the strength that God has given you. Write a declaration to remind yourself that you can do all things through Christ and it is His strength that empowers you in your times of weakness. Use your words and the word of God to ignite the drive and passion needed to push through in your walk to freedom.

Day 19

Quit Starting Over

"I do not consider, brethren, that I have captured and made it my own [yet]; but one thing I do [it is my one aspiration]; forgetting what lies behind and straining forward to what lies ahead, I press on toward the goal to win the [supreme and heavenly] prize to which God in Christ Jesus is calling us upward." – Philippians 3: 13-14 AMP

"Runners take your mark."

I can remember sitting on the edge of the sofa watching as a particular race was getting ready to start in the Olympics. All the months of training and discipline had come down to this moment and it was time for the runners to prove themselves.

"Get set."

I could feel the intensity as if I was in the race myself and couldn't wait for things to get underway.

The gun sounded and the runners took off. They battled for the leading position and one runner in particular seemed to be dominating the pack. It looked as if he had reached a comfortable stride and it was smooth sailing, but then the unthinkable happened…the runner tripped and fell. I could hear the collective sigh from the crowd and I thought for sure that his chances of placing were nonexistent. But I watched as the runner got up, got right back into stride and once again began fighting for position. He knew he had to dig a little deeper than the other runners to make up

71

ground and before long, you could see him pass one competitor after another. He kicked into another gear when the others seemed to be getting tired and to the shock and awe of everyone watching, ended up winning the race.

Now can you imagine if when that runner fell, he had to go back to the starting line and begin the whole race again? Living a life of freedom is just like that race that I watched so many years ago. There may be times when you stumble and fall, but there's a vast difference between starting over and restarting. To start over means having to redo everything you've already done, and when that leads to discouragement, which it almost always does, most people just give up. But when you restart, you're gathering yourself from right where you are, acknowledging that yes, there was a fall, but you're not out of the race.

In your journey to freedom, quit starting over! If you mess up, fine. If you react in a way that you said you'd never do again, so what?! It's one thing to continually do the same thing over and over, but we all stumble when we're first learning how to walk. The important thing is that you keep going with all the knowledge that you've gained and don't allow others, or even yourself, to make you feel like you've lost ground. The only time you lose is when you give up.

Your Work:

To close out this day, write your own declaration of encouragement to look back on in the times that you feel like you've fallen. This will be your reminder that you're not starting over, but you're picking yourself up from where you are, dusting yourself off and restarting on your journey to freedom.

Day 20

Reading and Reflection

Read Psalm 121 in its entirety. Afterwards, use this page as a journal entry to record your thoughts about this chapter and what it means to you.

Day 21

Refocus

"For the rest, brethren, whatever is true, whatever is worthy of reverence and is honorable and seemly, whatever is just, whatever is pure, whatever is lovely and lovable, whatever is kind and winsome and gracious, if there is any virtue and excellence, if there is anything worthy of praise, think on and weigh and take account of these things [fix your minds on them]." – Philippians 4:8 AMP

"I squint a little bit every now and then but overall I think my vision is fine." That's the line I gave the optometrist as he was examining my eyes. I admit I was a little overdue for my yearly eye exam (by a few years), but I wasn't having any major issues so I didn't feel the need to rush in. He finished the exam and told me he was writing me a different prescription and to go to another part of the office to pick up my new contacts. I didn't think it would make that much of a difference but I did as he said and put in the new lenses. The assistant informed me that it would take some time for my eyes to adjust, but that I should notice a significant improvement in my vision. I finished up my paperwork and could tell that the words looked a little clearer on the page, but it wasn't until I walked outside that reality truly hit. As I exited the building the green on the trees was a little bit greener, the lines in the parking lot were a little bit straighter and it made me realize that the vision to which I had become accustomed was more flawed than I wanted to admit. And then, the real work began.

Just as the assistant told me in the office, my eyes had to adjust to being able to see clearly. After years of squinting and ignoring the blur that was in front of me, my eyes were now doing the work of refocusing and translating the images that I saw. In the days that followed I had to get used to a new depth perception and even suffered from severe headaches because my focus was completely different. There were times when I had to take my new contacts out and just rest my eyes because the contrast was so great from what I was familiar with. After about a week and a half, I finally got to a point where the headaches stopped, everything that I looked at seemed normal and by this time, I no longer needed to rest my eyes from the refocusing. I became so adjusted to this clearer way of seeing and living and it became so comfortable for me that I would even forget to take my contacts out after several weeks and exchange them for a new pair. I don't know how I ever functioned with the way I was seeing before, but I'm glad that I went through the process of refocusing so that I could see clearly.

Have you ever heard the saying "you can't see the picture while you're in the frame"? Well, it's the same concept here. You never know just how much mess you're in until you get out of it…just like I didn't know how bad my vision was until it was corrected. We become so used to doing things a certain way and living in a certain manner that we don't realize just how off it really is. When we're finally able to separate ourselves from that situation or that way of thinking, we have to go through a process of refocusing. Yes, there may be pain involved. Yes, there will be new things that we have to get used to, but being able to see clearly is definitely worth it in the long run!

Your Work:

Make a comparison list of some things you used to focus on that were negative that you can replace with something positive. If you've been filled with hatred, try refocusing on love. If you've been dealing with a certain habit that you can't seem to break, try refocusing on the overcoming power you've been given through Christ. Make out your list and retrain your thoughts each day to focus not on where you are, but where you want to go.

Day 22

Secure Your Mask First

"Look well to yourself [to your own personality] and to [your] teaching; persevere in these things [hold to them], for by doing you will save both yourself and those who hear you." – 1 Timothy 4:16 AMP

"Oxygen and the air pressure are always being monitored. In the event of decompression, an oxygen mask will automatically appear in front of you... If you are traveling with a child or someone who requires assistance, secure your mask first, and then assist the other person." – *Air Odyssey Inflight Passenger Announcements*

Anyone who has been on an airplane has heard the routine safety warnings from the flight crew. They run through them like they're simply saying their name, but within these speeches lie vital instructions that when followed, could save your life and the life of someone else. But there's always that one that raises an eyebrow amongst most caring individuals, "secure your mask first". This goes against the instinctual concern that we have for others, especially children and those we feel are weaker than ourselves. But understanding what happens if we don't follow this instruction can help to shed light on its importance.

In the event that a plane loses cabin pressure while at altitude, the oxygen masks are deployed. During this time, a person has only seconds before the lack of oxygen will cause them to pass out, which if prolonged, could lead to serious complications or even death. So why wouldn't it make more sense to put the mask on a child first?

Because in the time it would take you to lay hold of the mask, secure it on the child, then try and secure one for yourself, you would have lost consciousness and there may not be anyone available to assist you. However, if you secure your mask first, even if the other person passes out momentarily, when you restore the flow of oxygen it will help them to regain consciousness with minimal to no damage. So, while it may seem selfish, it is imperative to your survival and those around you, that you ensure your safety before attempting to help anyone else.

Now, what does that tell you in your life of freedom? You can't take care of others until you first take care of yourself. So many times, we put ourselves in harm's way trying to help someone else, ignoring the danger that it causes to us. We stay in relationships and friendships because we feel the other person needs us or because we don't want to be replaced, all the while causing more and more damage mentally, spiritually, emotionally, and sometimes even physically.

It would be much more beneficial for ourselves and the other people in our lives if we FIRST make sure we are healthy and whole before we try and do anything for anyone else. It's hard for you to assist someone in a hospital if you are a patient yourself. The germs that you spread and those spread to you will only make each person's illness worse. Better to take the time that you need and get what you need than to realize after you've put everyone else's mask on that there's no oxygen left for you.

Your Work:

A little bit of selfishness is healthy when it comes to making sure you are happy, healthy and whole. Create a declaration giving yourself permission to put you first despite what anyone else may think, feel or express. You are worth it!

Day 23
Tunnel Vision

"Looking away [from all that will distract] to Jesus, Who is the Leader and the Source of our faith [giving the first incentive for our belief] and is also its Finisher [bringing it to maturity and perfection]. He, for the joy [of obtaining the prize] that was set before Him, endured the cross, despising and ignoring the shame, and is now seated at the right hand of the throne of God." – Hebrews 12:2 AMP

When I was younger I visited an amusement park with some friends and family. I hadn't yet developed my risk-taker persona and was a little too scared to ride any of the big roller coasters, so my friend suggested a ride that was calmer but still exciting for someone my age. We stood in line for what seemed like forever and the longer we waited the more excited I became. When it was finally our turn, we entered this cave-like building and had to get into a small raft that was floating on top of a few feet of water. The ride attendant gave us the safety instructions and told us we would have to paddle our way through the cave in order to come out on the other side. They handed us the paddles and sent us on our way, but I had no idea what exactly I was getting myself into.

For the first couple of minutes, everything seemed pretty cool. There were drawings and formations on the walls and some interesting sights to see. We were cruising along nicely, but then we crossed into another section and my heart nearly jumped out of my chest. Our pathway narrowed and instead of the sightings on the walls, there were now monsters and creatures, hissing, growling and grabbing at us. I remember screaming for dear life and in my moment of panic, I dropped the paddle that I was using to help

85

maneuver us through the cave and became paralyzed by fear. My friend was trying her best to steer the raft, but with me no longer paddling, it was harder for her to control our direction and we ended up going in circles. Everywhere I turned there was some grisly beast reaching towards me and all I could do was scream. We were so close to the end, but because I was focused on what was making noise and looking frightening around me, I was stuck…too far from the starting line to go back, but still unable to move forward towards the finish.

Eventually one of the park employees made it to where we were and spent the next few moments calming me down. When he finally got me to stop screaming, he told me to open my eyes and look at the creatures around me. I knew they weren't real, but I didn't want to look because I was terrified and just wanted to get out of the cave as soon as possible. But when I opened my eyes, I realized something even more important than the fact that these creatures weren't real…they couldn't touch me. No matter how scary they looked, no matter how loudly they hissed and growled, they could only come so far. After a few deep breaths and a lot of coaching, I was able to keep that fact in mind, focus on the light at the end of the tunnel and help my friend steer us to the other side of the cave.

Now how can this be applied to living a life of freedom? There are times when you may start off on the journey and things are smooth sailing. But then, all of a sudden you turn a corner and it seems like everything starts to come at you to make you fearful, cause distractions and knock you off course. In those times, it's important to develop tunnel vision and remember that fear is not real and distractions only have the power that you allow them to have. You have to determine in your heart and mind that no matter what comes at you, no matter what or who is making noise around you, and no matter how scary things look, your eyes are fixed on God and the future that He has for you.

Your Work:

Take some time now to write your own declaration to the fears and distractions that try to divert your attention from your goal. Whenever those things arise, come back to this declaration as a reminder to keep your eyes on the prize and to not let anything or anyone keep you from reaching the ultimate goal of complete and total freedom.

Day 24

Undercooked Process

[But what of that?] For I consider that the sufferings of this present time (this present life) are not worthy to be compared with the glory that is about to be revealed to us and in us and for us and conferred on us!" – Romans 8:18 AMP

When I was in college, I became a huge fan of microwavable meals. For breakfast, lunch, dinner and even a snack in between classes, I was always throwing something in the microwave for a quick zap. It was fast, easy and even though it could taste rubbery and have a few cold spots, it provided the nutrients I needed to get through the day. I spent my time in the grocery store looking at the backs of the packages and based my purchases on which meals would cook in the shortest amount of time. As I would glance at the cooking instructions, I always noticed that there was a section for a conventional oven, but looking at the time that would take, I couldn't imagine why anyone would wait over an hour for something that could be ready in five minutes.

As the years went by and I learned to cook a little more, I ate less of the frozen, microwavable meals, but I always kept a few on hand just in case. Then one night as I was relaxing at home, hunger hit and I didn't feel like going through the trouble of cooking a full meal. I pulled one of my backup, frozen dinners out of the freezer and since I had some time on my hands, decided to try it in the oven. I set the timer for the hour and a half that was suggested in the instructions and returned to the sofa to continue relaxing and finish the movie I was watching. The first thing I noticed was, unlike the cooked plastic smell that would come from the microwave, the aroma that filled the room as the dinner cooked in the oven, started to make my mouth water. Before long, my stomach was growling and I was anxiously awaiting the sound of the timer. When it finally went off, I jumped up like a kid on Christmas but knew I still had to give the meal time to cool before I could dig in. When I was finally able to take that first bite, I knew in an instant why someone would wait over an hour for something that could be ready in five minutes. This meal tasted like something that had come straight from my grandmother's kitchen. The meat was more tender, the vegetables were crispier and everything just seemed to melt in my mouth. After finishing off every bit of food on the plate, not only was I full but I was satisfied. In that moment, I realized that although the finished product may have been the same from five minutes in the microwave, the quality from the time in the oven made it so much better!

In the fast-paced world we live in, everyone wants the quick solution. Sometimes we feel like if the process is taking longer than we want, it must mean something is wrong. But as God is working in us and through us, we have to remember that it's for the quality that He wants to bring out of us. We can try to speed things up and may even get a similar result, but many times we're just left with something undercooked like frozen meat in a microwave.

Your Work:

Your assignment for today is to create a prayer to keep you focused in this process. Let God know that you trust Him and His timing in whatever He is doing and that the resulting quality of His work is your ultimate goal. Whenever you may get frustrated or feel like God is taking too long, come back to this prayer and pray it again and again. Make sure that you are doing your part, but leave the rest up to God. He knows what you have need of and on your journey to freedom, rest in the fact that your best interest is always His priority.

Day 25

Value the Inch

"Thank [God] in everything [no matter what the circumstances may be, be thankful and give thanks], for this is the will of God for you [who are] in Christ Jesus [the Revealer and Mediator of that will]. – 1 Thessalonians 5:18 AMP

Have you ever tried moving something that was too heavy for you to lift on your own but you couldn't wait for help, so you had to move it by yourself? I was rearranging a space at work and had everything in place, but there was a very large platform that I needed to move to the other side of the room. Now I'm pretty strong for my size so I was quite confident that I would be able to at least lift one side, which would make it easier to move. I didn't have much to grip but I bent down as far as I could to lift with my legs, not my back and with one big exhale and heave, I realized the platform was a lot heavier than it looked and there wasn't going to be any lifting going on. The only option I had if I was going to get it to the new position on my own, was to push it, one side at a time.

I started pushing with everything in me, but I could only slide the platform a few inches at a time, then I had to go pull in the opposite direction from the other side. I did this back and forth and at first it didn't seem like I was being productive at all...but I kept going. After what seemed like forever and a lot of energy, I could see that the platform was moving and getting closer to the position I wanted. It was such a tiring process and my body was already beginning to ache from all the strain, but I had done too much to quit and I was determined to finish what I started. Eventually all my pushing, pulling and rocking paid off and that big platform was on the other side of the room where I needed it to be.

Making any type of change in your life is the same as me trying to move that platform. If I had judged my success based on my ability to pick it up and carry it across the room, I would've labeled myself a failure. It reminded me of something I heard some years ago, "By the inch is a synch…by the yard is pretty hard". Many times when we're trying to do something different, we want to measure our progress in an instant or by some momentous occurrence. We get so caught up in the milestones that we negate the small victories which get us to the milestones. In times like these, it's helpful to remember that taking baby steps still means you're moving forward.

So, it's time to stop being hard on yourself because you haven't yet reached the yard, and give yourself credit for the inches of progress you have accomplished. You can make a complete 180 in a moment's time, but it's the small steps that get you to a destination in that new direction. You may not be where you want to be, but be grateful that you're not where you used to be.

Your Work:

Take some time now to value the inch. Make a list of changes you've been able to make, things you've been able to accomplish and lessons you've learned on your journey to freedom. If there's ever a time when you feel discouraged about your process, come back to this list and see just how much progress you've made. By the inch, you will get to the other side!

Day 26

Weather the Storm

"But as they were sailing, He fell off to sleep. And a whirlwind revolving from below the upwards swept down on the lake, and the boat was filling with water, and they were in great danger. And the disciples came and woke Him, saying, Master, Master, we are perishing! And He, being thoroughly awakened, censured and blamed and rebuked the wind and the raging waves; and they ceased, and there came a calm. And He said to them, [Why are you so fearful?] Where is your faith (your trust, your confidence in Me – in My veracity and My integrity)?..." – Luke 8:23-25 AMP

Have you ever seen a palm tree during a storm? Everyone marvels at the beauty of these trees in their tropical climate, but their most unique features are brought to light in the dangerous conditions that a storm can bring. To start, the root system of a palm tree, unlike other trees, is very compact and doesn't span out over a large area. These centralized roots are dense and serve as an anchor that weighs the tree down and holds it steady during strong winds. Next, the trunk is composed of bundles of vascular materials that provide water and nutrients and reinforce the stem, giving it flexibility which allows it to bend when gusts occur. Lastly, most trees have long branches with twigs and leaves attached forming something like an umbrella. During a storm or a windy period, this umbrella catches the wind and contributes to the tree being blown over, splitting it in half or even uprooting it at its base. On the contrary, a palm tree has no branches. Its long, evergreen leaves grow directly from the stem and instead of catching the wind, the wind blows through them in the same direction the tree is bending and they're more likely to return to their natural position afterwards. All these features make the palm a resilient structure in nature and give us a pattern that we should follow when the storms of our lives begin to rage.

As we check our root system, we have to make sure that our foundation is found in God and God alone. He gives us the density that we need to remain steady when tests and trials come. If your soul is anchored in Him, there's not any storm that will be able to uproot you or your purpose. Along with that strong foundation comes the flexibility to bend in the face of a storm, but not break. While people around you may be buckling under the pressure, not only will you be able to survive the harsh times, but the palm tree demonstrates the posture that you should take in order to make it through…a posture of prayer. As your prayer life grows, so will your strength to withstand what the world throws at you. Finally, be careful who you allow to connect with you because when the winds begin to blow, those connections will either flow with you as you submit to God or they'll contribute to making you fall.

Storms are inevitable. Many people feel like storms are there because they've done something wrong or because God is trying to punish them. But nowhere in the world is there a perfect climate where a storm never occurs. Jesus, Himself, went through a tumultuous time and had so much confidence that He was able to sleep through it, and when He was awakened, He spoke to it and caused the winds to cease. That same power rests in you. God didn't create you to break or be uprooted when trials come. He did, however, give you the power and authority to weather the storm and become even stronger as a result.

Your Work:

Tap into the power that God placed within you. Write a declaration establishing your root, your posture and the purpose of your connections. Use this declaration when storms start raging in your life so that you can remain steady on your course to freedom.

Day 27

Xenon Effect

"But let endurance and steadfastness and patience have full play and do a thorough work so that you may be [people] perfectly and fully developed [with no defects], lacking nothing." – James 1:4 AMP

When I was in middle school, I began learning about the periodic table of elements. At first it was difficult to remember the difference between atomic numbers, mass numbers, which one told the number of protons, neutrons, and even more importantly why I needed to know all that information. But as I progressed through school, what I had learned in the previous grade became easier and I was able to build the new concepts on a firm foundation of prior knowledge. Then one year, we went deeper than just memorizing numbers and symbols and actually began to study the properties of the elements on the table. Of all the groups of metals, nonmetals and gases, there was one element that, for some reason, stuck out to me then and has become significant to me as an adult.

Xenon is what's referred to as an inert, noble gas because generally, it is chemically non-reactive due to its atomic structure. I used to think it was a dud of an element if it couldn't form a compound but when I understood why, it shed a different light on it for me. Not to get too deep into chemistry, but elements form compounds based on the electrons they have in their outer orbital ring. If the outer ring isn't filled, the element will link up with another element that has similar empty spaces in order to fill them and a chemical compound will be formed. Xenon is among a group of elements that don't readily react because their outer ring is already filled, making them stable on their own. There are no empty spaces, so xenon doesn't

101

need another element in order to be complete. Although a chemical reaction isn't necessary, in the cases where it does combine with another element, the compounds are most commonly used in specialized light sources and medication for potentially deadly diseases.

So, when I think about the properties of xenon and how they relate to living a life of freedom, I'm reminded of the importance of being complete within oneself. Any time we have a struggle, a character flaw or simply a bad habit, it will attract people with similarities and we tend to link up with them because there is something lacking in our lives. Even if we consider ourselves to be introverted or disconnected from others, if we don't deal with our voids, we will be quick to react to situations and circumstances in ways that are usually detrimental to our well-being. Therefore, it is necessary that we take on the xenon effect. We have to become stable and whole within ourselves so that when we do connect with someone else, it will bring light, life and a compound that is beneficial to you and your journey.

Your Work:

It's time to put a property of a xenon compound into action. Create a prayer asking God to illuminate the voids that are present in your life and emotions. Within your conversation, ask Him to show you how to fill each of those voids and be content within yourself and your connection to Him. Remind yourself that He is your source of completeness and allow Him to stabilize you, fortify you and turn you into the element of His kingdom that He needs you to be.

Day 28

Yellow Light Warning

"Be well balanced (temperate, sober of mind), be vigilant and cautious at all times; for that enemy of yours, the devil, roams around like a lion roaring [in fierce hunger], seeking someone to seize upon and devour." – 1 Peter 5:8 AMP

So, I'm driving down the road, blasting music and trying my best to get to my destination on time. I've got a million and one things on my mind, so admittedly I'm distracted and not paying as much attention to the road and my surroundings as I should. I look up and see a yellow traffic light and have a split-second decision to make. I don't know how long the light has been yellow but I do know that I don't want to stop and delay my arrival any further. My lead foot commits to moving me forward and I speed through the light just as it's turning red, not realizing there's a police officer sitting on the other side of the intersection. It didn't take long for me to notice the blue lights in my rearview mirror and I just knew I had a ticket coming.

I pull over to the side of the road and get my license and insurance card ready. As the officer is approaching my car, I'm trying to prepare a face that would invoke sympathy and a way to express the importance of where I'm going so he'll show mercy. Before I could say anything, the officer looked at me and said, "Ma'am, I just saved your life". He proceeded to explain that he could tell I wasn't paying attention and at the speed I was traveling, it was only a matter of time before an accident occurred. He went on to joke that he knows, when people see a yellow light, they usually think to themselves *hurry up...a red light is coming*. But the light was designed to be a warning, when if ignored, can lead to a serious collision and cause harm not only to yourself, but to others as well. He lowered his sunglasses, looked me square in the eye and said, "You had time to stop, but you reached a point of no return simply because you were going too fast and not paying attention".

I know you're probably wondering if I got a ticket that day, but the more important question is what lesson came out of that experience? As we go through life, we all can be distracted by emotions, disappointments, struggles and sin. We get so wrapped up in what's going on with us that we ignore the warning signals that God is flashing right in front of our eyes to keep us on a safe path. Even if we see these warnings, some of us are so determined to do what we want to do in our timing and so fixed in a certain direction that we speed right through them. Yes, it's important to reach our destination, but there comes a time when you have to slow down and pay attention to what's going on around you. If not, God may just allow you to keep going until you reach that point of no return, setting yourself on a collision course that could lead to grave danger.

So now it's time for you to make a split-second decision. Many people think it's the enemy's job to stop us from reaching our destination, but he's much craftier than that. He places things in our path to distract and if we're not vigilant, we'll get caught up and eventually stop ourselves. But today you'll begin overcoming this tactic.

Your Work:

Find a quiet place where you can sit and not be interrupted. Now, focus on the destination that you're trying to reach. Once you have that in mind, think of all the things that seem to always pull your attention from that destination and make a list of them. Identify these distractions and equip yourself to recognize and deal with them accordingly so that your road to freedom can be one without any dangerous collisions.

Day 29

Zone In

"Put on God's whole armor [the armor of a heavy-armed soldier which God supplies], that you may be able successfully to stand up against [all] the strategies and the deceits of the devil. For we are not wrestling with flesh and blood [contending only with physical opponents] but against the despotisms, against the powers, against [the master spirits who are] the world rulers of this present darkness, against the spirit forces of wickedness in the heavenly (supernatural) sphere." – Ephesians 6:11-12 AMP

When I was younger, one of my favorite shows to watch on television was *American Gladiators*. Every week, two men and two women competed in a series of different events set up to test their physical strength, their strategizing ability and their sheer, unadulterated will. The crowd in the arena and millions watching cheered them on as they pushed themselves passed their limits for the chance to win a monetary prize and more importantly, the title of champion. But it wasn't enough that they only contend with each other, they also had to deal with bigger, stronger opponents, called gladiators, whose ultimate job was to stop them from reaching their goal. It was survival of the fittest and it all came down to one final event called the Eliminator.

Unlike all the previous events, which only had a singular goal, the Eliminator was made up of several different obstacles that each contender had to go through in the fastest time possible. The challenges may have varied from week to week but included tasks like climbing cargo nets, swimming underneath fire pits and leaping over walls. Then just as it seemed the contenders had reached a point of complete exhaustion, there was one final obstacle standing in between them and the finish line…a gladiator hell-bent on stopping them. These gladiators would wrestle them to the ground, pin them against walls and even throw oversized medicine balls at them in an effort to slow them down, trip them up and keep them from finishing the course. Out of all my years of watching the show, I witnessed a few contenders give up in these final moments, but the others knew they were only a few steps away from victory, so they zoned in on what they were fighting for, put their heads down and pushed through to the finish.

So, what's the correlation? Consider your road to freedom as the Eliminator. You're going to go through obstacles, you're going to have walls in your way and just as you approach the finish line, the enemy will be waiting and will do everything in his power to slow you down, trip you up and keep you from finishing your course. But in these final moments, you have two choices: you can give up because the obstacles are too much for you to overcome, or you can zone in on the future God has promised you, fix your eyes on Him and push through to your victory. Both you and these obstacles have a task to complete, but it's up to you which one is allowed to win.

Your Work:

If you've decided that your task is more important than any distraction that comes your way, it's time to declare it. Write a declaration that you will zone in and stay focused on what God has placed in front of you. Make statements that will keep your eyes set, your feet moving forward and your mind sure on the course of living a life free, indeed. These are the makings of a true champion.

Day 30

Forever Changed

In the Amplified Version of Romans 12:2, the Bible says, "Do not be conformed to this world (this age), [fashioned after and adapted to its external, superficial customs], but be transformed (changed) by the [entire] renewal of your mind [by its new ideals and its new attitude], so that you may prove [for yourselves] what is the good and acceptable and perfect will of God, even the thing which is good and acceptable and perfect [in His sight for you].

The last twenty-nine days have been a metaphorical renovation of the space in your mind. Some things have been cut away, some moved around or adjusted, and other things have been added or upgraded. It can be a messy process, during which you still have to live in and occupy the space, but you have the foresight to envision the outcome. Just like with any renovation, you can't control what the previous condition of the property was, but you do have total control over what it can become. This is your masterpiece! This is your opportunity to take everything that life has thrown at you and turn it into something that is good and acceptable and perfect in the sight of God for you!

On this last day of your renovation, it's time to close the book on how things used to be and open yourself up to a new way of living. You have the strength, the power and the wisdom that you need to live forever changed and construct the life that you desire for yourself. Looking back on this process from Day 1 until now, create a prayer that seals off the old and welcomes in the new. Allow this prayer to continue to change your mind as you walk out your journey to living free!

My Prayer for You

Father, I ask that You would be with each and every person reading this book. It is Your desire that we all live a life of freedom and I thank You that You are giving each reader the strength to do what is necessary to access that freedom for themselves. Some things may have been difficult, but You said in Your Word that You would never put more on them than they can bear. I thank You that even when things do get hard, that You are there to uplift them and uphold them with Your right hand. Father, open their understanding for them to know the full magnitude of Your love for them. Let Your gentleness, kindness, faithfulness, and tender mercies overtake them. Father, encourage them when the road may seem long and arduous. Station Your guardian and warring angels around them in all that they do. Send an ambush against any enemy that would try to stop them and their progress. Father, everything they have laid down in the last thirty days, I thank You that it will no longer have any influence on their future. Old things are passed away and behold, everything in them is made new in You. Thank You for new life! Thank You for a new outlook! Thank You that nothing will be able to negate the work You have done and will continue to do in their life! Today is the beginning of the best days they have ever seen and I give You glory for allowing it to come to pass. In Jesus' name I pray! AMEN!

If this book was a blessing to you, I invite you to connect with me.

A. Nicole Alexander/AleCo Enterprises LLC
1635 Old 41 Hwy NW
Suite 112-123
Kennesaw, GA 30152

(678) 822-6329
alecoplace@gmail.com

For more information, visit our Facebook page at:
www.facebook.com/alecoplace

www.ingramcontent.com/pod-product-compliance
Lightning Source LLC
Chambersburg PA
CBHW071135090426
42736CB00012B/2128